Images of His Beauty

A 10 week Bible study for young women desiring to find hope and healing in Jesus Christ.

Images of His Beauty

Published by Martus Press
© 2008 by Tracy Davis Steel

ISBN: 978-0-615-53611-8

Library of Congress Control Number 2011916192
Printed in the United States.

Credits:
Editor: Karen Lee-Thorp
Cover and Interior Design: Tekeme Studios
Cover Photo: Erin McFarland Photography

11   10   9   8   7   6   5   4   3   2   1

What others are saying about *Images of His Beauty*

"When the Apostle Peter referred to the "hidden person" of a woman, he was describing the quality that is "precious in the sight of God" (I Peter 3:4). Nothing is more beautiful than a daughter of the Heavenly Father understanding her beauty and from where it comes. Tracy Davis Steel has authored a way for a woman to make this discovery from the very Scriptures themselves. This study will be an adventure in wisdom."

–Dr. Darryl DelHousaye
President of Phoenix Seminary
Phoenix Seminary, Phoenix, Arizona

"This is an encouraging, insightful, and solidly Bible-based study that will help bring God's own presence and power into many women's lives."

–Wayne Grudem, Ph.D.
Research Professor of Theology and Biblical Studies
Phoenix Seminary, Phoenix, Arizona

"Scottsdale Bible Church has a unique support group. The amazing leaders of Images of His Beauty have encouraged young women recovering from eating disorders for 5 years. Time after time, women have told me how their IOHB group experience was transformational. Indeed, IOHB shortens the time women spend in 1:1 therapy."

–Nonie Maupin, MSW, LCSW, ACS
Minister of Lay Counseling
Scottsdale Bible Church

"The curriculum asks challenging questions and impacted me at a different level…Whether or not a person has an eating disorder, this is powerful stuff, and I grew throughout the ten weeks spiritually…it is an incredible comfort to know that I am not alone as a person who once had an eating disorder."

–IOHB Group Participant

Table of Contents

Dedication

IOHB is written for and dedicated to all young women who struggle with an eating disorder or with their self-image. Know that you are not alone and that IOHB was created for you. Our desire is for you to embrace Christ's love, thrill in how He has made you, and grasp that you are an Image of His Beauty.

Acknowledgments

Scottsdale Bible Church and its remarkable people contributed to the insights and wisdom expressed in this book. Special thanks to Nonie Maupin, Adele Goldstin, Kerry Grimes, and Enriqueta Turanzas for their participation in and support of this ministry.

All praise and glory goes to the Father, Son, and Holy Spirit, who truly authored and oversaw the creation of IOHB.

Scripture Abbreviations

Old Testament

Gen. *Genesis*

Num. *Numbers*

Jos. *Joshua*

1 Sam. *1 Samuel*

Ps. *Psalm*

Prov. *Proverbs*

Isa. *Isaiah*

Jer. *Jeremiah*

Mic. *Micah*

Zeph. *Zephaniah*

Mal. *Malachi*

New Testament

Matt. *Matthew*

Rom. *Romans*

1 Cor. *1 Corinthians*

2 Cor. *2 Corinthians*

Gal. *Galatians*

Eph. *Ephesians*

Phil. *Philippians*

1 Thess. *1 Thessalonians*

2 Tim. *2 Timothy*

Heb. *Hebrews*

1 Pet. *1 Peter*

Rev. *Revelation*

Session 1

Images of His Beauty (IOHB)

There is nothing better! You are adored by the God of the universe. You are special, beautiful, and are created for a specific purpose. Are you sure of this? Whether your answer is yes, maybe (on some days), or no, welcome to IOHB. You are about to embark on an exciting journey through God's Word. Our prayer is that you would open your mind and heart to hear what God wants to say to you. He loves you and wants you to find hope, healing, and freedom from the pain that your struggle with your self-image issue or eating has caused. Thank you for coming on this journey. Jesus never disappoints!

The goal of IOHB is to enable individual group members to grow in their knowledge of:

Images	I: Identity in Christ
Of	O: Overcoming through Christ
His	H: Healing through Christ
Beauty	B: Bearing the Image of Christ

If you have chosen to go through IOHB on an individual basis, you may skip session 1, because this session enables those who are going through IOHB in a support group to become acquainted with each other and familiar with how the group will function. Thus, you may begin by reading pages 15-16 and continue with the session 2 study that follows.

Or perhaps you are a young woman who has been battling an eating disorder, and you are seeking to find support to overcome and heal, so you have chosen to go through IOHB as part of a support group. We hope you will soon discover that you are not the only one who struggles in this way and that there are young women just like you! You are about to meet some godly women, your facilitator(s), who have been there and who want to provide you with support and encouragement through the study of God's Word, as well as prayer support. At the end of the ten sessions, we hope you will have grown in your knowledge of biblical truths, in your acceptance of how God created you, and in your understanding of ways you can display His beauty to the world around you. Are you ready to get started? The best place to start is with prayer. Let's begin our time as a group by asking God to move in our hearts and minds.

Take some time to pray about this study and for each person present.

In our first meeting, we'll learn what to expect in the upcoming weeks. Please turn to session 2 so you can preview how a typical group session will go. Some weeks will have specific memory/theme verses that correlate to the session, some will teach you a "spiritual tool" or practical spiritual discipline, and others contain a verse that you can personalize. Please note that the questions or activity for reflection at the end of the session are to be completed during the week following the session as homework. There are also blank "Jottin' the Journey" journal pages at the end of every session. You may use them to record answers to your homework, or for journaling. You will be expected to complete the homework and come prepared to share what you learned.

Now spend some time as a group reading out loud the following "Girls Rule!" guidelines. Please keep these in the forefront of your mind as you participate in the weekly meetings. These will help ensure that the meetings will run smoothly and be of benefit to you. By signing the Informed Consent form prior to the start of this meeting, you have agreed to adhere to the following to the best of your ability:

Girls Rule! #1: Be relevant. The only way you can play a significant role in this group and in your own healing process is by being here and showing up. You have agreed to attend all ten group sessions of this study. Remember to call your Group Administrator or facilitator if your absence will be necessary.

Girls Rule! #2: Be real. Please come ready to share what God is teaching you. Don't worry about what others will think; be honest with where you are at. Please don't share any graphic details about your eating disorder, and try not to compare or minimize what you or another group member is going through. We are here to heal!

Girls Rule! #3: Be respectful. You have agreed not to repeat anything that is said here. Allow everyone in the group to share. Be quick to listen and slow to interrupt as the other group members are sharing.

Girls Rule! #4: Be responsible. Please turn your cell phone off, and note that only bottled water will be permitted into the group meetings. Also remember that at the end of each session various questions or activities for reflection will be assigned. You will be held accountable for completing these on your own time and will be expected to discuss your answers with the group at the beginning of the following meeting.

Got it? Remember to refer to these "Girls Rule!" guidelines often. Now let's move on to the fun stuff . . .

Your facilitator(s) will share their testimonies and how they became interested in helping with IOHB. You'll learn what God has done and is doing to help them heal or grow in their relationships with Him. Afterwards, feel free to ask them questions about anything shared or discussed thus far.

Finally, let's take some time to find out a little about you. Don't worry, you don't have to share your deepest darkest secret! Just share the basic "4-1-1" on YOU:

- Your name
- What school you attend and grade level
- Favorite or desired vacation destination
- Hobbies or career goals
- Or, you may choose to discuss the more important topics of life: your opinion about vampire novels, which phone app you use the most and why, what your favorite reality TV show is and why—just have fun getting to know one another!

We look forward to seeing you again next week. Please make sure to bring a pen, a Bible, and this Participant Guide to the meeting. You can prepare for next week by reading Identity in Christ—the Lie, the Truth, the Challenge on pages 15-16. Keep in mind that the session 2 material that follows will be done as a group during the next meeting.

Close your time together by praying for the upcoming study and for each other. If you would like to share a prayer request pertaining to you personally, you may do so. Remember to pray for each other during the coming week and to keep all prayer requests and other information shared during the group meeting confidential. Have a blessed week!

Identity in Christ

Please read this section on your own before you meet again with your group.

Who are you? Do you know what your purpose in life is? Our purpose and our identity are critical things for us to figure out. Life can be confusing, and growing up can be hard. Change sometimes brings pain. Our hormones and our minds battle against us at times too! This leads us to look for answers. We hear one thing from our friends. We hear another from our parents. We watch TV shows and advertisements, or look at pictures in magazines to find another supposed answer to the questions raised above.

The Lie

Many people today believe that the company you keep and the possessions you own define you. For instance, they join a certain political, sports, or social group to help them define who they are and what they believe. Some look for the answer in a horoscope. Once they find out who they think they are, they set out to discover their meaning or purpose in life. Most people hope their purpose is to be successful and rich! They purchase a house, car, and acquire a line of credit—only to find out that they are now, ironically, a prime target for identity theft. Perhaps they lose their job or their health, or their home is robbed or damaged by a fire. Who are they now and what has happened to their purpose? So much can change in a short amount of time, and those who once defined themselves and their purpose based on fleeting relationships, careers, and possessions learn that it was useless to do so.

The Truth

Our identity does not stem from our job titles, salaries, possessions, or who we know. There is only One who does not change, One whose purposes for our lives will never be destroyed. The One is God. The truth is that God Himself never changes, and His Word, promises, and plans for us can never be taken from us. We are to look to Him alone to find the answers to our true identity and purpose.

During the next couple of sessions we will be studying God's Word to discover the truth about our identity and God's identity. By the end of the ten sessions, you may also have a better understanding of God's true purposes for your life as well.

The Challenge

People today are buying into the lie that their source of identity comes from something or someone in the world. As stated above, even other people can try to steal your earthly identity from you, but they can never steal your true and eternal identity. Similarly, just like the identity thief is stopped when the real person comes forward armed with the truth about his or her earthly identity, so the lies we have believed about ourselves are stopped once we come forward armed with the truth about our eternal identity.

Maybe you have struggled with an eating disorder or self-image issues for a while now and have begun this study feeling discouraged and defeated. It's time to uncover the real you—it's time to take back what has been stolen from you. It is time to face the TRUTH.

So again: Who are you, and what is your purpose?

Session 2
Identity in Christ: God Revealed

1. Welcome back! Let's start by looking at the issue of identity. On the previous page you were asked the following questions: "Who are you, and what is your purpose?" If you're doing this study with a group, please share with everyone your initial answer to these questions. Also, share one or two things mentioned in the lie/truth/challenge material that stood out to you and why.

Read the following theme and memory verses out loud. If you're meeting with a group, have one person read them. During the coming week, please review the verses daily on your own. As you review them, use the "Jottin' the Journey" journal found on pages 25-26 to record how God uses these verses to speak to you.

theme verse:
You have made them [humans] a little lower than the angels and crowned them with glory and honor. (Ps. 8:5)

memory verse:
I praise you [God] for I am fearfully and wonderfully made; your works are wonderful, I know that full well. (Ps. 139:14)

2. How do these verses speak to you—do they challenge or encourage you? Why?

Have one group member read questions 3 through 5 out loud. Then spend a few minutes sharing your answers. You may write your responses in the space below each question.

3. The verses above give us some insight about our true identity. What does the word identity mean?

4. Words I would use to describe myself (both positive and negative):

Words I would use to describe God:

5. What would God say about you if you were talking with Him face to face? In other words, what does God think of you? Do you think there's a difference between what God says about you and what you say about yourself? Explain.

Let's open God's Word and see how He describes Himself. There are a lot of opposing opinions out there about who God is. These can leave us confused and misinformed, and can lead us to turn away from Him when life gets hard. But we are now going to the source Himself. Whether we believe and accept the following truths is pivotal. Let's see what He has to say.

Look up the following verses to learn what they say about God. If you're meeting with a group, you can take turns reading the verses out loud. Please allow 20–30 minutes for this part of the study. Beside the list of verses is a brief summary of what the verses teach—these have been provided in case there is not enough time to read every verse aloud in the group.

6. Truths about God's identity:

God never changes.	Mal. 3:6; Heb. 13:8
God is good.	Ps. 100:5; 106:1; Luke 18:19
God forgives.	Ps. 103:8, 11-13; 1 John 1:9
God is beautiful.	Ps. 27:4
God is eternal and sovereign.	Isa. 46:9-10; Ps. 90:2, 102:25-27; Jer. 29:11; 1 Cor. 2:9; Rev. 1:8

(Eternal means He has no beginning or end. Sovereign means He alone is the One who knows and declares future events.)

God never lies, He is trustworthy.	Num. 23:19; 1 Sam. 15:29
God is love.	1 John 4:8

Have one group member read questions 7 through 10 out loud. Then spend a few minutes sharing your answers. You may write your responses in the space below each question.

7. Which of these truths, if any, are hard for you to believe about God? Why?

8. Which of these truths, if any, are easy for you to believe about God? Why?

9. Do you know anyone who always forgives, never lies, or never changes? If so, how do those qualities affect the way you relate to that person? If not, how does that affect the way you relate to people?

10. Does anything we've been discussing motivate you to turn to God first over others? If so what? If not, why not?

As we've discovered, we may have believed lies about the identity of God, our Creator. In addition, we can also struggle with our identity because we have become a prisoner to a stronghold in our mind. Throughout the upcoming sessions, you will learn about various "spiritual tools." These are additional disciplines you can choose to incorporate into your life that will help you grow in your daily walk with Jesus Christ and experience victory. Let's learn about the first one now.

 **Spiritual Tool #1:** Praying Scripture to help overcome strongholds

11. Read 2 Corinthians 10:3–5 out loud. Write down what it teaches about strongholds.

As we just read, if we are followers of Jesus Christ we have been given weapons with divine power to demolish strongholds. However, what is a stronghold? Is it a big deal? In *Praying God's Word*, Beth Moore defines a stronghold like this:

- A stronghold is anything that is exalted in our minds as greater or more powerful than God.
- A stronghold meets Satan's goal of taking our focus off God and His Word.
- A stronghold makes us feel enslaved and controlled.
- A stronghold robs us of the peace we gain from having the Master in control of our lives. [2]

For example, any of these could be strongholds:
- An obsession with being thin
- A craving to be rich and famous
- A habit of criticizing oneself or others
- A habit of using food to numb painful emotions

As you can see, being aware of strongholds is a big deal! They keep us from experiencing intimacy with God and from living the life He intended for us. They negatively affect us physically, mentally, and relationally. We must demolish them! Read on to discover what those divine weapons that demolish strongholds are.

Have one group member read questions 12 through 17 out loud. Then spend a few minutes sharing your answers. You may write your responses in the space below each question.

12. The war on strongholds is waged in the mind. Why do you think this is?

13. Read Ephesians 6:10–18 to find out about the weapons God gives us to fight strongholds. What are the weapons listed in this passage?

14. All the weapons listed are for us to defend ourselves, except one. Which piece of armor is the offensive weapon that God gave us for fighting back?

15. Elsewhere Scripture teaches that God's Word acts like a sword. Read Hebrews 4:12 out loud. According to this verse, what are two more things that God's Word does?

16. How then can we use the sword of the Spirit to help us fight against our struggle with an eating disorder or self-image issue?

In Ephesians 6:18, we are also commanded to pray in the Spirit. When we pray in the Spirit and use the Word of God (the Bible), we have the divine power to demolish strongholds! Isn't this great news?

17. Why do you think praying through the words of Scripture is considered to be an example of "praying in the Spirit"? (Hint: See 2 Timothy 3:16.)

Here's an example of how you can pray through God's Word. Read Psalm 73:25–26. You might pray:

God, I'm frustrated with my struggles, but I have hope because I know that You are good. You are so faithful to hear me, and You will never leave me. Help me to desire no one or nothing on this earth above You. Be my strength when my heart and flesh fail. Satisfy all that my heart longs for with You alone. I love You. Amen.

Pretty cool, isn't it, that words written two thousand years ago still speak to us and whatever we are going through! Praying through Scripture is a discipline you can also use to unleash God's power in the lives of those around you. You can pray Scripture over your own children someday, or over a loved one who is physically ill. Just try it and watch God work out His will and purposes (not just what you think is best) in their life. He says in Isaiah 55:11: "so is my word that goes out from my mouth: It will not return to me empty, but will accomplish what I desire and achieve the purpose for which I sent it."

You made it to the end of this week's lesson—way to go! Please take some time during this next week to read and answer the reflection questions below. May God continue to whisper His truth into your heart as you seek Him.

Questions for Reflection
(will be discussed with the group at your next meeting)

How do misconceptions about God's identity disconnect you from Him and possibly from others?

Can you identify a current or past stronghold in your life?

In what ways do you struggle with your thoughts? How do they affect your decisions?

Challenge: Personalize and pray through a scripture this week. How did it influence your thoughts or actions?

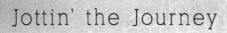

Jottin' the Journey

Before you begin the next session or meet with your group again, take some time to write down your reflections about the theme or memory verse. You may also use these journal pages to write your answers to the questions for reflection, or anything else you are experiencing on your journey with God.

"So do not fear, for I am with you; do not be dismayed, for I am your God. I will strengthen you and help you; I will uphold you with my righteous right hand." (Isa. 41:10)

Identity in Christ: A Treasured Temple

Welcome back! Open in prayer. Ask the Holy Spirit to help you understand and learn from the verses and questions below.

We hope you enjoyed jottin' down the beginning of your journey. God has probably begun to speak to you in some way. If you're doing this study independently, we encourage you to share with someone you love and trust how God is beginning to speak to you. The journey we walk with God can be exciting and challenging all at the same time—it helps to share it with someone along the way!

If you're going through IOHB in a group, take some time to share some of your reflections concerning the theme or memory verse, and share some of your answers to the questions for reflection from the previous session. Then move on to discuss questions 1 through 3 below.

1. If you were to walk up to random people on the street, what words do you think they would use to describe God?

2. Do you think their answers would match what we have studied so far? Why or why not?

3. Did anyone personalize and pray a Scripture passage this week? If so, which verse, and how did God use it to help you?

In this session we're continuing to talk about Identity. We'll focus on biblical truths about who we are and how God sees us as His sons and daughters.

In session 2 we jumped right into God's Word and learned how He describes Himself: as never changing, good, loving, forgiving, beautiful, sovereign, eternal, trustworthy and honest. Now let's turn the spotlight onto ourselves. In session 2 we jotted down how we describe ourselves and then how we think God would describe us. Are you ready to see how accurate your answers are? The following scriptures provide a small sample of what God says about you! May you be encouraged as the truth about your identity is revealed.

Look up the verses below to learn what they say about you. If you're meeting with a group, you can take turns reading the verses out loud. Please allow 20–30 minutes for this part of the study. Beside the list of verses is a brief summary of what the verses teach—these have been provided in case there is not enough time to read every verse aloud in the group.

4. Truths about your identity:

My body is a temple of the Holy Spirit and glorifies God.	1 Cor. 6:19–20
I am daily being conformed to the image of Christ.	Rom. 8:29
I am a child of God.	1 John 3:2
I was made in the image of God.	Gen. 1:26–27
My body is good, and fearfully and wonderfully made.	Gen. 1:31; Ps. 139:14

I am beautiful, for God is beautiful.	Ps. 27:4
God rejoices over my body— the way He created it to be.	Isa. 62:5; Zeph. 3:17
I am chosen to bear His fruit and to do good works that bring Him glory.	John 15:16; Eph. 2:10
I am righteous and holy; a part of a royal priesthood; a woman belonging to God.	Eph. 4:24; 1 Pet. 2:9–10

Have one group member read questions 5 through 9 out loud. Then spend a few minutes sharing your answers. You may write your responses in the space below each question.

5. Which of these truths, if any, are hard for you to believe about your identity and body? Why?

6. Which of these truths, if any, are easy for you to believe about your identity and body? Why?

7. Given your study of the verses above (and of those in session 2) which, if any, of your descriptions about God or yourself are distorted or twisted? How are they distorted?

8. As a result of our discussion today, do you view yourself or God any differently? If so, how do you view yourself now?

9. Despite what you may be feeling, what is your true identity? How would you describe yourself now?

Are you starting to see some of the lies you have believed about yourself or God? Sometimes we fear the truth, when in actuality the lies we believe can cause more pain and bondage than the truth! Sadly, some women live their whole lives believing that they are worthless, that they are not beautiful, or that God could never forgive them for sins they've committed. This is tragic. You don't have to be one of them. The list of scriptures presented here scratch the surface of what God has to say to you in His Word.

10. On your own now, please personalize the following verse by putting your name in the blank. Read it aloud in the privacy of your home this week until it sinks in and becomes part of you:

I (God) have loved _____with an everlasting love. (Jer. 31:3b)

You have now learned the truth about who and whose you are. Continue to study God's Word, hang in there, and cling to the truth of what God says. You are a child of God. You have a purpose. The fact that you are reading these words means you are a fighter!

In session 4 we'll learn that because of the cross of Christ, overcoming our struggle with an eating disorder or self-image issue is within reach. Do you believe this? Please prepare for session 4 by reading Overcoming through Christ—the Lie, the Truth, the Challenge on pages 35-36. Keep in mind that the session 4 material that follows will be done as a group during the next meeting.

Close your time together by praying for each other. Remember to pray for each other during the coming week and to keep all prayer requests and other information shared during the group meeting confidential. Have a blessed week!

Questions for Reflection

(will be discussed with the group at your next meeting)

Read John 15:1–11. What are the main things this passage teaches you? When is Jesus with you?

What steps can you begin to take today that will help you abide in Christ, so you can experience His joy and fruit, and overcome your eating disorder or self-image issue?

Jottin' the Journey

Before you begin the next session or meet with your group again, take some time to write down your answers to the questions for reflection. You may also use these journal pages to write down anything else you are experiencing on your journey with God.

"So do not fear, for I am with you; do not be dismayed, for I am your God. I will strengthen you and help you; I will uphold you with my righteous right hand." (Isa. 41:10)

Overcoming through Christ

Please read this section on your own before you meet again with your group.

In sessions 2 and 3 we've learned the truth about our identity and the truth about God. Despite what you've learned, you may discover that there are still things in your life that prevent you from becoming all that God calls you to be. They may keep you from experiencing the life Christ desires for you. Over the next couple of sessions we'll look at several obstacles that need to be uncovered and overcome so that true healing can occur.

The Lie

The following phrase: "I am woman, hear me roar!" was once a popular slogan. More than just a passing fad, this concept fed into many women's egos. It influenced the thoughts/beliefs that many women live by. We believe we are invincible, unstoppable, and in control of every aspect of our lives. We don't need anyone or anything to help us. The world was created for us to rule—hear us roar! All of the power is within us. We don't need some distant God or some religious set of rules to help us. Sound familiar? Yet how many women are tired, stressed out, depressed, and in bondage to guilt and shame? The world and Satan keep whispering in their ears: "You are woman—roar—you can have it your way." Sadly, women are falling for the lies, only to discover that they aren't the ones roaring. They are the ones being devoured. So what is a woman to do?

The Truth

Holding onto false expectations of ourselves and others can actually put us into bondage. However, when we stop "roaring" and release these expectations, we'll be set free from our bondage to them (Gal. 5:1). There are times when life seems out of control and if we don't do something, all will be lost. The truth is, God promises that no matter what happens He is in control and will be with us. He has not given us more than we can handle (Isa. 40:28–31; 41:10; 43:2).

The Challenge

Women weren't meant to roar. Maybe instead the slogan should be "I am woman, see me love!" Let's leave the roaring to God. When He opens His mouth and exerts His power, all obstacles we give to Him in faith will not stand. Are you ready to unleash His power to help you overcome? If so, put on your new image, for the old one does not define you anymore.

Session 4
Overcoming through Christ: Intimacy Restored

If you're going through IOHB in a group, take some time to share some of your answers to the questions for reflection from session 3. Also, share one or two things mentioned in the lie/truth/challenge material that stood out to you and why. Then move on to discuss questions 1 and 2 below.

1. When you read the word overcoming, what do you think it means?

2. Have you overcome another struggle or stronghold in your life? If so, would you be brave enough to share with the group or with another trusted individual what it was and how you overcame it?

This session will focus on overcoming our struggle with self-image or an eating disorder. We'll study biblical truths that teach us how to overcome our battles through the power and strength of Jesus Christ. He is the key to overcoming. However, we sometimes struggle with allowing Christ to help us overcome our battles. Feelings of shame, guilt, or not being forgiven by God can keep us from allowing God to help us. To be clear, God is all powerful and can accomplish anything He wants in our lives. He doesn't need our help. Through His mercy and grace He may choose to let us be a part of the miraculous work He is accomplishing in our lives. How thrilling is that? But can we hinder or not cooperate with Him? Absolutely! We, not He, can make overcoming our battles a longer and more painful process. Are you currently hindering or helping God in your battle to overcome?

Read the following theme and memory verses out loud. If you're meeting with a group, have one person read them. During the coming week, please review the verses daily on your own. As you review them, use the "Jottin' the Journey" journal found on pages 43-44 to record how God uses these verses to speak to you.

theme verse:
In the same way, count yourselves dead to sin but alive to God
in Christ Jesus. (Rom. 6:11)

memory verse:
There is now no condemnation for those who are in Christ Jesus,
because through Christ Jesus the law of the Spirit who gives life has
set you free from the law of sin and death. (Rom. 8:1–2)

Have one group member read questions 3 through 5 out loud. Then spend a few minutes sharing your answers. You may write your responses in the space below each question.

3. Wow—did you get what these verses are saying? What are a couple of things that jumped out at you as you read them?

4. How do these verses challenge or encourage you, and why?

Are you condemning yourself for your eating disorder behaviors or for some other sin pattern in your life? If you have put your faith in Jesus Christ and have trusted

Him for your salvation, condemnation of yourself is futile! However, does that mean you're free to continue to sin or harm your bodies if you're saved? Of course not, or as the apostle Paul wrote in Romans 6:1–2, "May it never be!" God has forgiven you, through the precious death and sacrifice of His Son Jesus on the cross. You are not stuck in your sins, but alive in Him. Do you want proof?

5. Read John 8:36 out loud. What do you think this verse means? What does freedom from an eating disorder or self-image issue look like to you?

6. Read aloud the following verses about God's forgiveness. Which of these do you struggle with, and why? Which ones encourage you, and why? Take time to write down what the verses say as each verse is read.

Ps. 103:12–13

Isa. 38:17; 43:25; 44:22

Jer. 31:34

Mic. 7:19

Acts 3:19

Rom. 10:9-11

1 John 1:9

If you struggle with feeling forgiven, you are not alone. In fact, Scripture records an account of a man who knew Jesus personally and yet struggled to receive the forgiveness Jesus offered him. In the end he was restored to Jesus, and the Holy Spirit used him to write some of the New Testament books of the Bible that we can study today. How awesome is that? God's grace is truly amazing!

Have one group member read the following Bible passages and questions 7 through 11 out loud. Then spend a few minutes sharing your answers. You may write your responses in the space below each question.

7. Read John 13:36–38. What promise did Peter make to Jesus?

8. Read John 18:15–18, 25–27. What happened? Was Jesus' prediction about Peter in John 13 correct?

9. Read John 21:4–8, 15–19. How do you think Peter felt after he betrayed Jesus? (See Matthew 26:75.)

10. What did Peter do when he saw the resurrected Jesus?

11. Peter went on to write the words found in 1 Peter 1:3–7. Write down what these verses say.

Peter was well acquainted with trials and being tested. Yet he survived to the glory of God, and so shall we! Peter did not let his shame or guilt keep him from loving and pursuing a relationship with Jesus! Jesus didn't push him away! He restored him and said, "Follow me" (John 21:19).

Is this true for you, today? Are you running toward Jesus or pushing Him away because of guilt or shame?

Thank you for persevering through what could have been a very difficult lesson this week. Discussing our shame and guilt can be uncomfortable. Realize, however, that feeling guilty is sometimes an internal warning sign that something is not right. Thus, feeling guilty may at times be beneficial! Just remember that we who are dead to sin and alive in Christ are not to dwell on feelings of guilt. Dwelling on guilt prevents us from moving forward in our lives and from overcoming our eating disorder or self-image issue through Jesus Christ. He has set us free.

Do you feel "free indeed"?

Questions for Reflection
(will be discussed with the group at your next meeting)

Do you struggle with accepting forgiveness from God for your eating disorder or for other sin(s) in your life? If so, journal about the areas you struggle with, and what you think might be keeping you from accepting what God offers.

Does shame keep you from turning to God (Isa. 44:22)? If so, journal your thoughts, asking God to forgive you and to take your guilt or shame away. Ask Him to do this despite how you may feel.

Next time you struggle with your self-image issue or eating disorder behavior, what can you do differently?

Jottin' the Journey

Before you begin the next session or meet with your group again, take some time to write down your reflections about the theme or memory verse. You may also use these journal pages to write your answers to the questions for reflection, or anything else you are experiencing on your journey with God.

"So do not fear, for I am with you; do not be dismayed, for I am your God. I will strengthen you and help you; I will uphold you with my righteous right hand." (Isa. 41:10)

Session 5

Overcoming through Christ: Fashioned for Battle

Welcome back! Open in prayer. Ask the Holy Spirit to help you understand and learn from the verses and questions below.

If you're going through IOHB in a group, share some of your reflections concerning the theme or memory verse, and some of your answers to the questions for reflection from the previous week. Then move on to discuss question 1.

1. What are you currently doing to help overcome your self-image issues or eating disorder?

This week we will continue to focus on overcoming through Christ. Last week we learned that a big obstacle in overcoming is often our own guilt and shame before God. We will now study some other obstacles that prevent us from overcoming our struggles through Christ. They are the flesh, the world, and the devil.

There are a variety of different English translations of the Bible. In some translations, the Greek word for flesh is rendered as "sinful nature" or "sinful desires" in verses where it doesn't refer to our bodies. As we discussed in session 3, our bodies are not bad or evil, but are "fearfully and wonderfully made." Our flesh is our lower nature, the part of us that rebels against God.

Likewise, in the passages we're studying in this session, world refers to human culture insofar as it is hostile to God and His ways. It doesn't mean non-Christians. Jesus tells us to love our enemies and those who persecute us (Matt. 5:43–45), but we must not love the values of a culture when they clash with God's values. We can try to serve the world and serve Jesus, but one will ultimately gain our devotion—be aware of this and choose wisely!

Discuss questions 2 through 7 with your group, and record your answers in the space below.

2. Take turns reading aloud 1 Peter 2:11–12; Romans 7:14–25; and Galatians 5:17–24. What do they teach you about the flesh or sinful nature?

3. Take turns reading aloud John 15:18–19; Colossians 2:8; 2 Timothy 3:1–5; and 1 John 2:16–17. What will we face as we try to follow Christ out in the world?

4. Take turns reading aloud John 8:44; 1 Peter 5:6–11; and Revelation 12:9–10. What do these passages teach about the devil or Satan and how he works against you?

5. Thankfully, God doesn't leave us helpless to defend ourselves against the flesh, the world, or the devil! Take turns reading aloud Romans 8:5; 2 Corinthians 10:5; and Galatians 5:16. How can you have victory over the flesh?

6. Take turns reading aloud John 16:23, 33; Romans 12:2; 1 John 5:3–5; James 4:4; and 2 Peter 1:3–8. How can you have victory over the world?

7. Take turns reading aloud Ephesians 6:10–18; James 4:7; and 1 John 4:4. How can you have victory over the devil?

It is pretty encouraging to learn that we can have victory over these, isn't it? Let's revisit Ephesians 6:10–18 and learn another discipline we can incorporate in our lives to help overcome our eating disorder or self-image issue.

 **Spiritual Tool #2:** Putting on the armor of God

Have one group member read questions 8 and 9 out loud. Then spend a few minutes sharing your answers. You may write your responses in the space below each question.

8. As you've read, Ephesians 6:10–18 describes putting on the full armor of God. For review, what are the specific pieces of armor listed in that passage?

Here's a challenge for you: Every morning during the coming week, "put on" the armor of God. How will you do this? Come back next week ready to share how you did it and how putting on the armor affected you.

9. Why do you think it's important to put on the armor of God daily?

We can try to keep overcoming our sinful habits on our own. Or as God's Word teaches (John 15), we can abide in Christ and allow Him to help us through the armor He has fashioned for us. A soldier is foolish to go into battle without a helmet, bulletproof vest, or weapon. Let's wise up and go back into our battle armed. You want to win, don't you?

10. On your own now, please personalize the following verse by putting your name in the blank. Read it aloud in the privacy of your home this week until it sinks in and becomes part of you:

_____can do everything through Him who gives me strength.

(Phil. 4:13)

Please prepare for session 6 by reading Healing through Christ—the Lie, the Truth, the Challenge on pages 51- 52. The session 6 material that follows will be done as a group during the next meeting.

Questions for Reflection
(will be discussed with the group at your next meeting)

What accusation does Satan want to play over and over in your mind?

What effects of your past sin(s) or eating disorder would you like to overcome through Christ's help?

Give them to God in prayer or a letter right now. He is waiting to help you! Ask God to help you battle against feelings of shame or guilt, or to help you against the world, your flesh, or the devil. You may write your letter to God on the following pages.

In all these things we are more than conquerors through him who loved us. For I am convinced that neither death nor life, neither angels nor demons, neither the present nor the future, nor any powers, neither height nor depth, nor anything else in all creation, will be able to separate us from the love of God that is in Christ Jesus our Lord. (Rom. 8:37–39)

Jottin' the Journey

Before you begin the next session or meet with your group again, take some time to write down your answers to the questions for reflection. You may also use these journal pages to write down anything else you are experiencing on your journey with God.

"So do not fear, for I am with you; do not be dismayed, for I am your God. I will strengthen you and help you; I will uphold you with my righteous right hand." (Isa. 41:10)

Healing Through Christ

Please read this section on your own before you meet again with your group.

Not many people enjoy being sick. Not many enjoy pain. Yet, as a result of the sin that Adam and Eve committed in the garden, sickness entered into the world. It wasn't originally supposed to be this way. We weren't supposed to need healing.

The Lie

Today Americans spend a lot of time and money researching and purchasing prescription drugs and over-the-counter quick fixes. Many look to science alone to cure them of all sorts of physical, emotional, and mental pain or sicknesses. In fact, some of these "cures" do take away the pain for a short time, and are not bad in themselves. Unfortunately, they often produce more questions, allergic reactions, or other side effects, and can leave millions of people in debt, frustrated, fearful, and discouraged. Many buy into the lie that life is about total happiness and that suffering is to be avoided and eradicated at all costs. Many also believe that man himself has the power to cure and to take away the pain. But does he?

The Truth

Scripture teaches that God alone is our Jehovah-Rapha, our Healer. It also teaches that He is bigger than cancer, heartburn, and yes, even eating disorders! Even when we are suffering, God promises that His grace is sufficient for us. And He promises a good and eternal purpose for all of the suffering and pain we encounter (James 1:2–4; 2 Cor. 12:7–10).

The Challenge

The Great Healer in His mercy and love for us provided the very best treatment to save us from ourselves and from the sickness of our sin. His health plan consisted of sending His one and only Son to die in our place as a payment for our sins. Indeed the greatest health remedy available to all who believe, and are sick, is the cross of Christ.

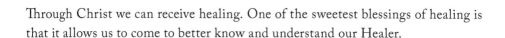

Through Christ we can receive healing. One of the sweetest blessings of healing is that it allows us to come to better know and understand our Healer.

In fact, your Healer is always on call to assist you. Do you want to know and understand Him better? Then get going, it's time for your appointment. The Great Physician is waiting for you.

Session 6

Healing through Christ: Point of the Process

If you're going through IOHB in a group, take some time to share some of your answers to the questions for reflection. Also, share one or two things mentioned in the lie/truth/challenge material that stood out to you and why. Then move on to discuss questions 1 and 2 below.

1. Did you attempt the armor of God challenge? If so, what happened?

2. Reflect on the last week. In what ways have you overcome some of your past? How do you feel about this?

This session will focus on the process of healing. We will study biblical teaching that affirms that through Jesus Christ we can experience true healing from the effects of our self-image issues or eating disorder. As with overcoming, Christ is also the key to true emotional, physical, and spiritual healing for those who come to Him for help!

Please read the following theme and memory verses out loud. If you're meeting with a group, have one person read them. During the coming week, please review the verses daily on your own. As you review them, use the "Jottin' the Journey" journal found on pages 57-58 to record how God uses these verses to speak to you.

theme verse:
Come to me, all you who are weary and burdened, and I will give you rest. (Matt. 11:28)

memory verse:
Praise the LORD, my soul, and forget not all his benefits—who forgives all your sins and heals all your diseases. (Ps. 103:2–3)

Besides helping you overcome, God also promises to help you heal! Have one group member read the following Bible passages and questions 3 through 7 out loud. Then spend a few minutes sharing your answers. You may write your responses in the space below each question.

3. Read Psalm 30:2; 147:3. What do these verses say about healing?

4. Read 1 Peter 2:24. What does this verse teach about healing?

5. Is it hard for you to cry out to the Lord? When you do, what does He promise to do for you, His child? Can you think of a time when He has done this?

6. What do you think being healed from your self-image issue or eating disorder will look like or mean to you?

7. Now that you realize that God is your Jehovah-Rapha (God, my Healer), what are you going to do differently?

Are you encouraged by what you're learning? You may have entered into IOHB discouraged. You may have tried many different medications, or completed several hours of therapy but found yourself still in bondage and in pain. While medications can be effective and therapy sessions helpful, these things by themselves can't cause complete healing and freedom from our self-image issue or eating disorder. Jesus Christ is the only One who can. He may choose not to heal you as quickly as you'd like Him to, and if He chooses not to, there's always a reason why. That is why we must persevere in our faith and trust Him. His healing often comes in a process. Could it be that in the process of becoming healed, you might just come to know and love your Healer more? Maybe, just maybe, that's His reason for taking His time. Many women who once struggled with eating disorders or self-image issues found Jesus through their pain. They weren't sorry they did, and neither will you be.

Activity for Reflection
(will be discussed with the group at your next meeting)

Read Isaiah 40—41. These two chapters tell of the greatness of God and how He wants to be the strength behind our healing. Select and personalize sections of the chapters and write them on the following pages. Or you can select another passage that speaks to you in some special way. Meditate on this passage throughout the week, and when you meet for session 7 share how God spoke to you.

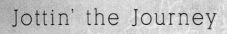

Jottin' the Journey

Before you begin the next session or meet with your group again, take some time to write down your reflections about the theme or memory verse. You may also use these journal pages to write about your reflection activity, or anything else you are experiencing on your journey with God.

"So do not fear, for I am with you; do not be dismayed, for I am your God. I will strengthen you and help you; I will uphold you with my righteous right hand." (Isa. 41:10)

Session 7

Healing through Christ: Mastered by God Alone

If you're going through IOHB in a group, take some time to share some of your reflections concerning the theme or memory verse, and share some of your answers to the activity for reflection from the previous session.

Now that we have learned that God plays a part in our healing process, we must also do our part in the healing process by being good to our body, because it is a holy temple. The apostle Paul writes,

> *Do you not know that your bodies are temples of the Holy Spirit, who is in you, whom you have received from God? You are not your own; you were bought at a price. Therefore, honor God with your bodies. (1 Cor. 6:19–20)*

Scripture teaches several ways that we can honor God with our body. By speaking words that are truthful and that encourage others, we can honor God with our mouth. When we provide goods or services to those less fortunate, we honor God with our hands. When we abstain from sex before we're married, we honor God with our bodies. When we read Scripture, books, or watch movies that promote Christian values, we honor God with our eyes and minds. When we display the fruit of the Holy Spirit in our lives, we use our whole self to honor God and bring Him glory.

Have one group member read the following Bible passage and questions 1 through 3 out loud. Then spend a few minutes sharing your answers. You may write your responses in the space below each question.

1. Read Galatians 5:22–23. List the fruit of the Spirit mentioned here.

2. While time does not permit us to study each fruit in depth, we will focus on the last fruit mentioned, self-control. How would you define self-control?

3. What does self-control look like in our thinking and eating habits?

In *Living Beyond Yourself*, Beth Moore writes, "It is not God's will for us to be mastered by anything other than Him. He wants us to be free . . . from the obsession of eating and from the obsession of not eating."[3]

4. Spend the next five minutes in silent prayer, asking the Holy Spirit to help you grow in the discipline of self-control. Ask Him to help you live out self-control in the ways you listed above as it pertains to your eating or thinking habits. You may write your prayer to Him in the space below and revisit it often this week if you wish.

Like a city whose walls are broken through
is a person who lacks self-control. (Prov. 25:28)

The walls that were built around ancient cities protected them from being conquered by enemies. Movies love to depict battle scenes where the attackers find or make a hole in the outer city wall to weaken it. We then watch as the attackers bring the walls down, eventually running through them and bringing devastation to whomever is inside. The tide of battle usually turns at this point. However, the good guys still usually win!

What a great description of what can happen to us if we lack self-control! We have enemies too—we learned about them in session 5.
Do you remember them? (Fill in the blanks below).

Our enemies: the f_____, the w_____, and the d_____.

Beware. If the devil can find a weak spot or an area of temptation in your life, and you aren't practicing self-control, you may fall! Always stay on your guard. We will never arrive or be beyond needing the Holy Spirit's help daily to live in a way that honors God. Knowing when to say "no, I will not ____" is part of growing in godliness. If you ever feel that the enemy has broken in and you're losing ground, call out to God for help. He doesn't like to lose. He never will! The end has already been written. Praise Him!

5. Check out the ultimate battle and what happens in the end. Have one group member read aloud Revelation 20:7–10; 21:1–22:5. Discuss what these verses say and how they make you feel about God and what is to come. Do you think that this same God is able to help you achieve ultimate healing and victory over your struggle with eating or self-image issues? If so, why? If not, why?

6. Do you feel forgiven and believe that you can overcome and heal through Jesus Christ, or are you still struggling? Explain how you're feeling with the group. Or if you're going through IOHB individually, consider talking with a trusted friend or family member about where you are at so they can pray with or encourage you. This week's study is shorter than the rest to allow as much time as needed for the group to discuss this question and to pray with those who are struggling with feeling unforgiven or who are struggling with overcoming and healing in general.

Thanks for hanging in there and tackling some tough topics over the past several weeks. We've looked at the truths about who we are and realized we've fallen prey to some lies that need to be replaced so we can love God and ourselves more. We've had to discover, deal with, and work to remove feelings of guilt or shame because of our struggles with eating or other areas of sin. We've become aware of the destructive nature of our flesh, the world, and the devil and have been equipped for victory against them so we can overcome. And we have learned the precious truth that our healing can never come from our own strength but from our Jehovah-Rapha, who is ready to answer when we call. Finally, by relying on the Holy Spirit and walking in self-control, we can grow in wisdom and win the battle. Is your head spinning yet?

In session 8 we move into our last section of IOHB, where we'll learn about bearing the beauty of Christ's image. The more you grow in godliness, the more you display His beauty to the hurting world around you. True beauty comes with a price, and the beauty of what Christ did for us on the cross is priceless. The world needs to hear about this beauty. Will you share it with them?

Please prepare for session 8 by reading Bearing the Image of Christ—the Lie, the Truth, the Challenge on pages 65-66. The session 8 material that follows will be done as a group during the next meeting.

Questions for Reflection
(will be discussed with the group at your next meeting)

Are there any other areas of life that you need to exercise self-control in? If so, what are they?

Revisit the list of spiritual fruit in Galatians 5:22–23. Are there some that grow from you easily? Are there others that are more difficult? Write a prayer asking the Holy Spirit to help you bear more of this fruit. Ask Him to help you to have more self-control in the other areas of life you listed above as well.

Jottin' the Journey

Before you begin the next session or meet with your group again, take some time to write down your answers to the questions for reflection. You may also use these journal pages to write down anything else you are experiencing on your journey with God.

"So do not fear, for I am with you; do not be dismayed, for I am your God. I will strengthen you and help you; I will uphold you with my righteous right hand." (Isa. 41:10)

Bearing the Image of Christ

Please read this section on your own before you meet again with your group.

Up to this point in our study, we have learned the truths about our identity and about our power to overcome and to heal through Jesus Christ. As we enter our final weeks together, it's time to turn our focus outward—to realize that people around us are also hurting.

The Lie

Every little girl at some point in her life has wondered, "Am I beautiful?" These little girls grow up and spend a lot of time and money to make sure that the external answer to this is yes!

Why is all of this money spent on cosmetics, surgical procedures, tanning, and fashion? Could it be because women believe that external beauty fulfills their need to be loved, respected, or accepted? Some women would probably answer yes. While there are numerous answers to this, the money is spent because our culture is selling lies about true feminine beauty, and women are falling for them.

The Truth

The truth is that varicose veins, wrinkles, cellulose, hair on your chin will happen! Scripture teaches that physical beauty is fleeting (Prov. 31:30); therefore we are to pursue an internal and unfading beauty that pleases God (1 Peter 3:3–5). Since we are created in His image, true beauty is already ours. It is time we unleash it to the world around us.

The Challenge

In Joshua 24:15, God challenges His sons and daughters to "choose for yourselves this day whom you will serve." In Deuteronomy 30 He sets life and death before those He loves and asks them to choose. The choice before them is simple: obey

God and live according to the truth, or disobey God and follow the lies of the world. The choice is before you now, too. Will you continue in bondage to the lies that you have believed, or will you overcome and heal through Jesus Christ and bear His image? Whom will you serve?

Other women are buying into lies. They need to hear the truth—they need Jesus Christ to help them overcome and heal from their own struggles. It is time for you to help them. Yes, you! It is time for you to discover your true beauty, and it's time for you to bear His beautiful image to the world.

While you're at it, go ahead and throw out the fashion magazines—you won't need them anymore!

May God himself, the God of peace, sanctify you through and through. May your whole spirit, soul and body be kept blameless at the coming of our Lord Jesus Christ. The one who calls you is faithful, and he will do it. (1 Thess. 5:23–24)

Session 8

Bearing the Image of Christ: Unfading Beauty

If you're going through IOHB in a group, take some time to share some of your answers to the questions for reflection. Also, share one or two things mentioned in the lie/truth/challenge material that stood out to you and why. Then move on to discuss questions 1 and 2 below.

1. Would you describe beauty as something that remains the same, increases, or fades over time? Why?

2. When you read the phrase *bearing the image of Christ*, what do you think it means?

This week we will continue our final section of IOHB—the study of bearing the image of Christ. We will be focusing on the biblical truth that as Christ's daughters and sons, we bear or display His image to the hurting and dying world around us. No matter how we have hurt or struggled, or no matter what we have done or said to ourselves or others, God still has a purpose for our lives. He still loves us and sees us as beautiful, not because of our external features, but because we were made in His image. As we learned in session 2, He is beautiful—therefore we are beautiful just as He is! It's time to pick ourselves up and go out into the world and shine for Him!

Read the following theme and memory verses out loud. If you're meeting with a group, have one person read them. During the coming week, please review the verses daily on your own. As you review them, use the "Jottin' the Journey" journal found on pages 75-76 to record how God uses these verses to speak to you.

theme verse:
Put off your old self, which is being corrupted by its deceitful desires; to be made new in the attitude of your minds; and . . . put on the new self, created to be like God in true righteousness and holiness. Follow God's example, therefore, as dearly loved children. (Eph. 4:22–5:1)

memory verse:
Your beauty should not come from outward adornment, such as braided hair and the wearing of gold jewelry and fine clothes. Instead, it should be that of your inner self, the unfading beauty of a gentle and quiet spirit, which is of great worth in God's sight. (1 Peter 3:3–4)

Have one group member read questions 3 through 7 out loud. Then spend a few minutes sharing your answers. You may write your responses in the space below each question.

3. The world defines beauty in a way that contradicts what God and His Word says about beauty. How does the world define beauty or a beautiful person?

4. Has the media lied to us in any ways about what it means to be a woman? If so, what are some of their lies?

5. Why do you suppose the media's primary focus on women centers on their physical appearance and not on healthy living or motherhood?

6. What can we as a group do to guard ourselves from believing what our culture of thinness teaches us?

7. How do you think God defines beauty or a beautiful person in the Bible?

Have one group member read the following text, Bible passage, and questions 8 through 11 out loud. Then spend a few minutes sharing your answers. You may write your responses in the space below each question.

In the Old Testament book of Proverbs we get a lengthy description of an ideal woman who shared her God-given beauty with her family and those around her. Read Proverbs 31:10–31.

8. What are some of the characteristics that the Proverbs 31 woman possesses?

9. What do you think is important in God's eyes when He looks at the Proverbs 31 woman?

10. Why does the world's view of a woman/wife/mother make it a challenge to believe what the Bible tells us about our beauty and value?

11. Does the Proverbs 31 woman focus more on herself or others? Explain.

The benefit of focusing on others is that it takes the focus off ourselves. Those of us who struggle with self-image issues or an eating disorder can become self-focused or obsessed with ourselves at times. By turning our focus onto others and by giving our time and gifts to help them, we have less time to focus on our negative thoughts or to act out our eating disorder behaviors. Thus, others will benefit from our God-given beauty.

Have one group member read the following Bible passages and questions 12 and 13 out loud. Then spend a few minutes sharing your answers. You may write your responses in the space below each question.

12. Read Philippians 2:3–4. What does this passage tell us to do?

13. If we value others more than ourselves, we will be like Christ. Read Philippians 2:5–8. How did Christ show that He valued others more than Himself?

One of Jesus Christ's most beautiful characteristics was His humility. He emptied Himself and bent His knee to the point of death so we could be saved. One day all of us will bend our knees to Him and confess that He is indeed Lord of all and worthy to be praised. Can you even imagine something more beautiful than this?

To conclude today's lesson we will learn another way we can begin to become content with the way God has made us. One way to keep from letting the world define us and our God-given beauty is to take our thoughts captive to Christ. The following is a practical tool that will help you to do so.

Spiritual Tool #3 The "STOP" card[4] —Taking our thoughts captive to Christ

14. Have one group member read these passages out loud and write down what they say.

2 Corinthians 10:3–5

Philippians 4:8–9

The verses above focus on your thinking, on making your mind captive to Christ. How can you do this practically? You can begin by paying attention to what you read, listen to, and watch. What message are these books, images, and words sending you? Are they positive or negative messages about yourself? If they're negative, get rid of them, change the channel! This may be hard, so ask a trusted friend, family member, or pastor to help you do so. You can do this!

Also, purchase a packet of 3x5 index cards. Take one card, and on one side of it write STOP. On the other side write the following verse:

Finally, brothers and sisters, whatever is true, whatever is noble, whatever is right, whatever is pure, whatever is lovely, whatever is admirable—if anything is excellent or praiseworthy—think about such things. Whatever you have learned or received or heard from me, or seen in me—put it into practice. And the God of peace will be with you. (Phil. 4:8–9)

Then continue to pay attention to your thoughts during the week. Whenever you have a thought that comes through your mind that pertains to your identity or body, take a moment to STOP and mentally evaluate your thought through the filter of Philippians 4:8. Is this thought true . . . is this thought noble . . . is it right or pure or admirable? If it isn't, try to stop dwelling on this thought and do something to help your mind move on.

Most of the world's messages are defeating and inspire thoughts that aren't true. When we become more aware of our thoughts, we may realize they don't hold up to God's desire for our thinking. We must STOP these thought patterns and take them captive by turning the thought around to what is true, or to what aligns with Scripture. Therefore, the more Scripture we know, the quicker we'll know what is true, pure, lovely etc.

You may want to make several of these STOP cards and keep them in your purse, locker, Bible, or bedside table. Then you can STOP and use the card during the week whenever you start to feel defeated, ugly, etc.

Even though you're filling your mind with truth, there will still be times where you feel ugly or bad. That's okay; it can take time for feelings to change. In addition, Scripture teaches that sometimes our hearts (mind, will, and feelings) are deceitful (Jer. 17:9). Over time, truth-filled thinking will change your feelings. Not only will you know you're beautiful, but you'll feel it as well. What do you do with your true beauty? Next week you'll find out!

Questions for Reflection
(will be discussed with the group at your next meeting)

Do you compare yourself to your friends or family members? Why?

Challenge: Pray for the other person's well being when you find yourself tempted to compare.

What external influences make you unhappy about just being you?

Challenge: Ask yourself this week, "Whose approval am I seeking?" Journal on how this influences you.

What are some ways you can help yourself move on from a destructive thought?

Challenge: Identify and write down all destructive thoughts that you frequently have. After you've identified the recurring thoughts that don't meet the Philippians 4:8 filter, make additional STOP cards. Write STOP on one side and a verse that will redirect your thought or encourage you on the other side. Put the cards in places you will see as you go throughout your day. At the next session, share how this affected your thoughts.

Jottin' the Journey

Before you begin the next session or meet with your group again, take some time to write down your reflections about the theme or memory verse. You may also use these journal pages to write your answers to the questions for reflection, or anything else you are experiencing on your journey with God.

"So do not fear, for I am with you; do not be dismayed, for I am your God. I will strengthen you and help you; I will uphold you with my righteous right hand." (Isa. 41:10)

Session 9

Bearing the Image of Christ: Releasing Control

Welcome back! Open in prayer. Ask the Holy Spirit to help you understand and learn from the verses and questions below.

If you're going through IOHB in a group, take some time to share some of your reflections concerning the theme or memory verse, and share some of your answers to the questions for reflection from the previous session. Then discuss question 1.

1. How can you grow as a godly woman who is focused on your inward appearance, not your outward one? Offer as many ideas as you can think of.

In this session we'll see that no matter what we've done in our past, with Jesus Christ's help we can begin to live and think and behave in a new way. It's time to let God take control of our image and to be reflections of His beauty to those around us. It is time to pick ourselves up and go out into the world and shine for Him!

Have one group member read questions 2 through 6 out loud. Then spend a few minutes sharing your answers. You may write your responses in the space below each question.

2. If you are not to bear the world's image of a woman, whose image will you bear?

3. Given what we've studied thus far in IOHB, what do you think that means or looks like?

4. How does the truth that you bear God's image make you feel?

5. Does it change the way you see and treat your body? If so, how?

6. Are you ready for God to take control of who you are becoming, and help you reflect His image more and more? If not, what holds you back?

7. Take the next five minutes to write a prayer to God in the space below, asking Him to take control of who you are becoming. Give Him your dreams, fears, and how you see yourself now. He can handle it and is a great listener! (See Matt. 11:28–30.) Ask Him to help you surrender daily to His design for your life.

Have one group member read the following bodies of text and questions 8 through 13 out loud. Then spend a few minutes sharing your answers. You may write your responses in the space below each question.

8. Would you like to see an example of a woman whose beauty is still talked about today? This woman's name is not mentioned in Scripture, but the simple act she performed touched the heart of Jesus. Take a moment to read Luke 7:36–50. Have someone read the passage out loud if you are going through IOHB in a group format.[5]

9. Do you think it was a mistake that God chose not to tell us her name? Although she is nameless to us, she was never nameless to Jesus. He knew her name and all about the choices she had made. In fact, these verses don't describe her sins in detail. They tell us only that she had many of them (7:37, 47). Can you relate? Explain.

One might assume that these sins brought with them some painful consequences. Maybe they caused her physical or relational pain. The Pharisee wanted to send her away because of them. Jesus reacted the opposite way. Even though her sins were many, she was allowed access to her Savior and her love moved Him. So does ours.

10. Revisit Jesus' response to this event in Luke 7:40–50. Before Jesus talked directly to the woman, He had something to say to Simon the Pharisee. Summarize what they discussed in verses 40–47 in the space below, and then share what you wrote with your group.

11. What was the main lesson Jesus wanted Simon (and us) to learn from His parable?

12. Next, revisit Jesus' response to this unnamed woman in verses 48–50. Summarize what He said to her in the space below, and then share what you wrote with your group.

13. Unfortunately, Scripture does not tell us how she responded to hearing Jesus say, "Your faith has saved you; go in peace." If you were her, what would your response be?

Think again about your answer to question 13. Maybe it will shock or encourage you to realize that we are like this woman. We have also committed many sins. Through the free gift of God's grace, we have been saved through our faith in Jesus Christ (Eph. 2:8–9). Like her, Jesus is telling us to go, and to go in peace.

Amazing, isn't it! Scripture has shown us the perfect example of a woman who faced a choice: either continue in rebellion and reject God, or be transformed into what God wanted her to be—a forgiven woman at peace with herself and at peace with her Savior. The choice was hers. Scripture doesn't tell us what happened to her as she left Jesus' presence that day. It's doubtful that she left unchanged, for true encounters with Jesus always produce change.

As you've gone through IOHB, have you encountered Jesus? The choice is up to you. Do you want His peace? How will you live your life going forward?

Have one group member read the following verses and questions 14 through 16 out loud. Then spend a few minutes sharing your answers. You may write your responses in the space below each question.

14. Not only did God have a plan for this particular woman's life, but He has a plan for you too. One famous passage that is often quoted is Jeremiah 29:11–13. Look up this passage and read it out loud. What is God's plan for your life?

15. How does this verse make you feel?

16. How can the Lord use your past to glorify Him? How can you show Christ's beauty to the hurting world around you? Record some specific ways in the space provided below. Strive to actually do them in the days and years that follow! Take a couple of minutes to pray individually to the Lord for direction and strength to do so.

17. On your own now, please personalize the following verse by putting your name in the blank. Read it aloud in the privacy of your home this week until it sinks in and becomes part of you:

Being confident of this, that he who began a good work in _____ will carry it on to completion until the day of Christ Jesus. (Phil. 1:6)

To conclude this session we will learn another spiritual tool that will cultivate beauty in our hearts, a beauty that will inevitably spill out of us and onto those around us.

 Spiritual Tool #4: Praying with a heart of thanksgiving

Praying with a heart of thanksgiving is commanded in Scripture. Read out loud Philippians 4:6. As you may know, our prayers can consist of petition, adoration or praise, and thanksgiving. Not only does God want us to ask Him for provision and praise Him for who He is, but He also loves it when we thank Him for what He has done or will do in our lives.

He has been moving in the past nine weeks—it's time to remember and thank Him for doing so. Praying with thanksgiving changes our hearts. We encourage you to make this a regular part of your prayer life going forward.

18. Take the next five minutes to stop, pray, and thank God for the changes you have seen occurring in your life through IOHB. If you are going through IOHB with a group, pray out loud as a group so everyone can hear the specific ways God has been working in everyone's lives.

We have so much to be thankful for, don't we? As Americans we live in a country where we are free to live, buy, eat, and worship where and when we please. Yet so many people are unhappy and are dying without having a relationship with Jesus Christ. Just think the difference each child of God would make if she daily showed love, patience, peace, humility, or kindness to those around her? More people would become curious about Jesus because His image that we portray to them is inviting and accepting. Jesus created you to be beautiful, to have purpose. Start living it out; the world will notice and your heavenly Father will be pleased. He's quite taken with you already. It's time for others to be too.

Questions for Reflection
(will be discussed with the group at your next meeting)

What do you wish would be written about your life, or how do you want to be remembered?

Challenge: Pick a day next week, and turn every prayer that day into a prayer of thanksgiving. Example: Do you need to do well on a test? Pray, "Thank you, God, for the opportunity and the abilities I have as a student . . ." Journal on how this affected your thinking.

Jottin' the Journey

Before you begin the next session or meet with your group again, take some time to write down your answers to the questions for reflection. You may also use these journal pages to write down anything else you are experiencing on your journey with God.

"So do not fear, for I am with you; do not be dismayed, for I am your God. I will strengthen you and help you; I will uphold you with my righteous right hand." (Isa. 41:10)

Session 10
Next Steps with Christ

If you're going through IOHB in a group, take some time to share some of your answers to the questions for reflection.

Congratulations—you have completed Images of His Beauty. You should be proud of all the hard work and soul healing you did over the past ten weeks. We hope you're not the same as when you first opened this book. You have been prayed for and know that God is not finished shaping you into the woman He wants you to be. Even if you have only experienced a little change in your thinking or behavior as a result of IOHB, it's still a victory—so celebrate it! This study only scratches the surface, so continue to pray and to dig even deeper into God's Word for the rest of your life. May you thrill in the complexity and mystery of His love letter, the Bible, to us!

This session takes an overview of all that you've learned. Don't skip or hurry through the questions. It's good to review what you've learned so you don't quickly forget it.

If you're going through IOHB with a group, take some time to look back through the previous weeks' lessons. As a group, discuss any questions or verses that particularly challenged or encouraged you. Discuss any that you would like to review again or that you need to have clarified.

Have one group member read questions 1 through 6 out loud. Then spend a few minutes sharing your answers. You may write your responses in the space below each question.

Identity in Christ

1. What are some of the truths we learned about ourselves and about God?

2. What are some things we can do with these truths to make a difference in our own lives and the lives of others for the glory of God?

Overcoming through Christ

3. How would you define overcoming and what it looks like in regards to your eating disorder or self-image issue?

4. Name the emotions we may feel as a result of our sin(s).

5. Name the three enemies we learned about that prevent us from being able to overcome.

6. Do you still struggle with these enemies? Do you feel that since you began this study God has started to give you victory over some or all of them? If no, why? If so, how? Be specific.

7. Spend some time in prayer either as a group or individually (if time permits) thanking God for the victory you have experienced! He is so worthy to hear our thanks and praises—celebrate how far you've come and how hard you've worked! Way to go!

Have one group member read the following bodies of text and questions 8 through 10 out loud. Then spend a few minutes sharing your answers. You may write your responses in the space below each question.

Healing through Christ

We learned that God is our Jehovah-Rapha and promises to help us heal. We acknowledge that healing is a process, and that growing in the fruit of self-control is an absolute must for us. We believe that God hears our cries for help and that He has a reason for our pain.

8. Do you feel that you are growing in your knowledge and love of your Jehovah-Rapha? If so, how has this affected you? If not, why do you think this is, and what is holding you back? Would you be so bold as to share this with your group or another trusted friend so they can be praying and encouraging you?

Bearing the Image of Christ

We learned that true beauty as defined by God is not the same beauty that the media and world promotes. We looked at the Proverbs 31 woman and the woman who anointed Jesus' feet as examples of women who touched the lives of those around them with the beauty God gave them.

9. What are some of the ways you plan on giving yourself a spiritual "makeover" in the months ahead? How do you plan on sharing your true beauty with others?

10. Do you think you're beautiful? It's okay to say yes, but if not, why do you think you still struggle? Would you be so bold as to share this with your group or another trusted friend so they can be praying and encouraging you?

11. To conclude your IOHB study, spend as much time as you need in prayer thanking God for His love, for His truth, for what He has and will continue to do in your life. If you're in a group, spend as much time as you need lifting each other up, and in thanking God for this group. He loves to spend this time with His precious daughters. He is crazy about you! In fact, remember the quote at the beginning of session 1 that included the words "nothing better"? There is nothing better. We are adored by Him.

God's love message to you as you take your next steps with Christ:

"Forget the former things;
do not dwell on the past.
See, I am doing a new thing!
Now it springs up; do you not perceive it?
I am making a way in the wilderness
And streams in the wasteland."
Isaiah 43:18–19

May you let go of the former struggle you faced. God is good and is continuing to do a new thing in your life (Phil. 1:6). Believe it! Do you perceive it? May God flood your desert places with His healing power. And never forget that you will always be an Image of His Beauty.

Jottin' the Journey

Take some time to write down your reflections about the key things you learned from IOHB, or anything else you are experiencing on your journey with God.

"So do not fear, for I am with you; do not be dismayed, for I am your God. I will strengthen you and help you; I will uphold you with my righteous right hand." (Isa. 41:10)

We are so thankful that you have agreed to facilitate an Images of His Beauty (IOHB) support group. We hope that by the end of the ten weeks, group members will be able to understand and communicate how God wants them to use their struggle with an eating disorder for His glory. Perhaps they will be future leaders of IOHB themselves!

The following pages contain everything you will need to help you prepare for and facilitate IOHB. You will find:

1. A "Facilitator Training Material" section that equips pastors, counselors, or lay leaders in local churches to effectively lead the weekly meetings.

Included in the last portion of this section are the spiritual and character qualities required of those involved in an IOHB support group: its facilitator(s), group administrator, and group members. For IOHB to run smoothly and effectively, we believe that those participating in any capacity in IOHB must possess or be growing in the spiritual and character qualities outlined below for their particular role.

2. Various Consent/Commitment Forms. These forms are to be signed by IOHB group members prior to the start of the first meeting. They can sign the forms located on pages 105-110, tear them out, and turn them in to their group administrator or facilitator before the start of the first meeting. These forms assure that everyone participating is on the same page, so everyone involved in IOHB must be familiar with the information contained in these forms. The forms also enable the group administrator and facilitators to hold group members accountable should a problem arise (such as unexplained absences or a breach of group confidentiality).

3. An assessment tool. It can be hard to discern if a young woman is a good candidate for IOHB. We have included a tool to help you assess her status. Please refer to and use the "IOHB Informal Assessment" on pages 103-104 before allowing anyone into IOHB. If a young woman is not currently under the care of a licensed Christian counselor for her eating disorder, or is in deep bondage and needs to seek help for her eating disorder for the first time, IOHB is not the right fit for her. If you are not a professional counselor and are unsure about a potential IOHB group member, please seek the counsel of your pastor or of a professional counselor in your area.

Now that you have the tools to begin IOHB at your church, how do you get started?

- Pray! (For God's blessing and direction over IOHB)
- Fill the role of an IOHB group administrator.
- Fill the roles of the IOHB facilitator(s). Use your church bulletin or website as needed.
- Use the Facilitator Training Material to train IOHB facilitators.
- At the end of the training session(s), set dates for your IOHB meetings. IOHB is a ten-week support group. Each meeting should run approximately 2 hours.
- Advertise and fill the roles of the IOHB group members. Use your church bulletin or website as needed.
- As discussed above, assess potential IOHB group members.
- Distribute IOHB books to those who passed the assessment. Have them sign and turn in the various consent forms prior to the first IOHB meeting.
- Pray!
- Begin the group meetings and watch God and His Word bring healing!

May God richly bless the ministry He has given you. Healing from an eating disorder is a process. God's Word will not return to Him void and will accomplish

all that He has purposed for it in the weeks to come (Isa. 55:11). As long as a woman has the desire to overcome and allows the power of God's Word to enter her heart and mind, she will continue to overcome eating disorder tendencies. Nothing is impossible where our God is concerned. She will become an Image of His Beauty to a world that is hurting. May you thrill in watching Jesus transform her!

Facilitator's Training Material

Step-by-Step Procedures for Facilitating Small Groups

- Group facilitators may choose to bring extra Bibles, ball point pens, and a box of tissues to the meetings for the group members to use if needed. Feel free to bring in any other devotionals, Scripture passages, craft projects, or videos that you feel would enhance the curriculum as the Lord leads. However, please make sure the material is God honoring and aligns with the teaching of Scripture.

- Prior to the participant's arrival, the facilitators should pray for the group.

- Once the group time begins, open with prayer. Use the Session 1 instructions on pages 11-14 to help you lead the introductory meeting. A set of "Girls Rule!" guidelines are included there. These compliment the information contained in the Informed Consent Forms below that group members have agreed to abide by. You may choose to read the guidelines out loud at the beginning of every meeting to ensure that all those participating are on the same page.

- Please note that during the first meeting, facilitators are to share their testimony and how they became interested in helping with IOHB. Please limit your sharing to no more than ten minutes and don't include any graphic or disturbing details. You will want to highlight what God has done and is doing to help you heal or grow in your relationship with Him. Be sure to glorify God when sharing.

- For the remaining nine lessons, be sure to review the material prior to the meeting, using it to facilitate group discussion.

- At the end of the meeting, remind group members of their assignment for the next session and ask if they have questions.

- Take prayer requests and spend time at the end of the session praying for each member. Encourage the members to pray for each other throughout the coming week.

- After participants have left, facilitators should spend time discussing any concerns, questions, or praises. Discuss the upcoming meeting and who is leading.

Additional Things to Keep in Mind

- Try not to have a fixer mentality. Please stick to the curriculum, do not probe, and remember that eating disorder recovery is a process.

- Don't let members in the group try to fix one another. We want to have an atmosphere of grace.

- Get behind their eyes. Remember what it was like to be a young woman in high school, college, or post college. Try to understand their world and culture before making judgments or giving counsel. Empathize with their individual situations.

- It's okay if a member cries. Ask permission before you touch or hug a group member.

- If you would like to meet with members outside of group time for one-on one mentoring you may do so, but this is not required. Know your boundaries and don't be afraid to set them with a group member. (For example, no phone calls after 9:00 p.m., or you're available to meet twice a month outside the weekly meetings.)

- Your time commitment as a facilitator is to attend all of the facilitator meetings/training sessions and all of the ten weekly meetings.

- Prayer is an essential part of IOHB. Throughout the week, don't forget to pray for your fellow leaders and the group members.

- Aim to have balanced sharing during the group meetings. If one member is a talker, politely steer her back to the topic of discussion and tell her that you would love to hear more at a later time, then redirect the conversation. Reiterate at the start of every meeting that everyone gets to share. No one is to dominate the conversation.

- Don't be afraid of silence after you ask a question. The group members may need time to process the question. Be patient. Silence is okay.

- Don't allow members to share eating disorder behavior details. You can remind the members by saying, "Thank you for your honesty. Please remember when you share to use the term 'eating disorder behavior' instead of describing the specific activity." You never know who may be triggered by listening to another's story.

- Don't be afraid to share your own testimony or stories with the group members. The more open you are, the more they will be! Or share someone else's testimony or story (without using their names). Sometimes stories are the most powerful tool for reaching someone else.

- When a group member shares that she is depressed or hopeless or some

other deep emotion, empathize with her by saying, "You know I have felt hopeless before too. Why don't you call and talk to your counselor tomorrow about this." Don't probe or try to fix her emotionally. If you feel led, you may want to pray for her before you get back to the curriculum. Or if you feel it's something that needs follow-up later, talk to her after the meeting has ended.

- Do the same if a group member admits that she is active in her eating disorder again, cutting, or suicidal. Don't stop the group to ask details of how she's doing it or how often. However, it's okay to ask something like, "How did your actions make you feel?" Then move on. Ask to speak to her afterward one on one. If you feel led, you can pray for her and then get back to the curriculum. When speaking to her in private, remind her that you will have to break confidentiality because she is harming herself or possibly other people by her actions. Ask if she is currently seeing a counselor. If so, she needs to call her counselor and inform them of what has happened. Also let her know that if she is under 18 years old, her parents will be contacted as well. Pray with her and encourage her before you go. Always end on a positive note. Document what she said, and call the IOHB group administrator so they can contact the appropriate parties. The group administrator should then assess if the group member should be removed from the group. This should be decided on a case-by-case basis.

Questions a Member May Ask

- Why did God allow me to have an eating disorder if He is good and loving?

- I ask Him to help me recover, but He doesn't seem to be answering. Why not?

- Do you still struggle with your eating? (Group members will listen and may want to probe deeper into personal things you share, so don't go there if you don't want them to ask.) Remember not to share unnecessary graphic details.

Listen, empathize with their struggle, and direct them to the biblical truths of God.

Who Is Involved in IOHB

Spiritual and Character Qualities of an IOHB Facilitator:
- Authentic and growing relationship with Jesus Christ
- Desire to live a godly lifestyle evidenced in words, thoughts, and actions
- History of a past struggle with an eating disorder is desirable
- Committed and faithful to the IOHB ministry
- Organized and willing to lead the weekly lessons as asked by the group administrator
- A loving and empathetic heart for young women battling eating disorders

Spiritual and Character Qualities of an IOHB Group Administrator:
- One who has an appointed or recognized leadership position in a local church. This could be a full or part-time position, such as youth pastor, church counselor, director. Or it could be a lay leader who has direct accountability to church leadership—to the youth pastor, elder board etc.
- Desire to live a godly lifestyle evidenced in words, thoughts, and actions
- Committed and faithful to the IOHB ministry
- Organized and willing to train and follow up with the facilitators. Willing to carry out all administrative tasks in an IOHB ministry, including the ordering of IOHB books, advertising literature, assessment of potential facilitators and group participants, etc.
- A loving and empathetic heart for young women battling eating disorders

Spiritual and Character Qualities of an IOHB Group Member:
- Complete and pass assessment by the IOHB group administrator, pastor, or Christian counselor
- Responsible to fill out and turn in the following forms before the start of the first meeting: Consent to Interview and Disclosure of Information Form (pages 105-106) and the Informed Consent/Group Commitment Form (pages 107-110)
- Desires to heal from her eating disorder
- Open, honest, humble, teachable, and able to maintain group confidentiality
- Committed to attend all of the weekly meetings
- Desires to complete all weekly homework and memory verses as assigned

IOHB Informal Assessment[6]

Because of the seriousness of eating disorders, we require most participants to be in counseling while they go through the IOHB support group. Some women are far enough in their journey that this is not necessary. However, some do need the professional support. This is for the participant's health and safety. Isolation and secrecy are major aspects of an eating disorder. When a woman breaks the silence, her problems may increase. Therefore, a professional counselor is a necessary and supportive adjunct to her group experience. Not only that, she should be able to identify her healing journey thus far, in spite of how far she has to go.

As you begin your interview, get acquainted with her before you ask about her personal history. You may tell a shorter version of your own testimony before you ask for her story. Also, ask her what motivated her to attend this support group, and if she has any general questions about Images of His Beauty. Whether she's under a professional counselor's care or not, the following are just a few questions you need to cover.

- Ask her about past abuse and where she is on her healing path. If she reports a history of abuse, it's important that she's emotionally healthy enough to withstand her experience of strong emotion. Does she have some coping skills to handle strong feelings?

- Is she currently practicing her eating disorder behavior? Ask for specifics in regard to her eating disorder behavior. She should not be practicing eating disorder behaviors, for the most part. Most who join IOHB struggle primarily with their thought life in regard to eating.

- Is she currently involved in a relationship that could be considered

physically, sexually, or mentally abusive? Is she currently going through any type of personal crisis? If she is, then one-on-one counseling is preferable.

- Is she currently abusing recreational drugs, prescription drugs, or alcohol? This program will not help if this is occurring. She can attend a Celebrate Recovery or AA-related program. After she is sober 90 days, she can be evaluated for an IOHB group.

- Is she currently considering harm to herself or others? It's important that she's at a better place emotionally, in order for her to gain help from this group. Also, the group will require her to sign an agreement not to harm herself or others. If she expresses plans pertaining to suicide or expresses the intent to harm another person, IOHB will not be beneficial to her. If suicidality is a problem, she should seek immediate assistance from a suicide hotline or professional counselor. If you learn that she is imminently going to harm herself or others, you are morally obligated to call and state her threats to authorities. You do not need her permission to do so.

Consent to Interview and Disclosure of Information Form
Images of His Beauty Support Group

Images of His Beauty is a church-based ministry to young women who have struggled with eating problems and who desire additional support during their recovery. IOHB is led by adult Christian women who offer support and encouragement through various means, such as devotionals, group discussions, and prayer support. In ten weeks, group members will grow in their knowledge of biblical truths that will hopefully help them accept how God created them and in how they can demonstrate His beauty to the world.

We require anyone entering this support group to submit to a brief interview, in order to determine if the ministry will be beneficial. You will be asked for a brief description of your history with an eating disorder. A brief synopsis of your information will be given to the facilitators of IOHB and to the IOHB group administrator(s) in order to better serve you.

Your emotional, physical, and spiritual well-being are of utmost importance to us. Therefore, we are committed to your care and to the confidentiality of all personal information shared with us. Your identity and personal information will be protected and released only to the IOHB facilitators and to the IOHB group administrator(s).

I acknowledge that I was informed that a brief synopsis of my history of eating problems will be released to the IOHB facilitators and to the IOHB group administrator(s).

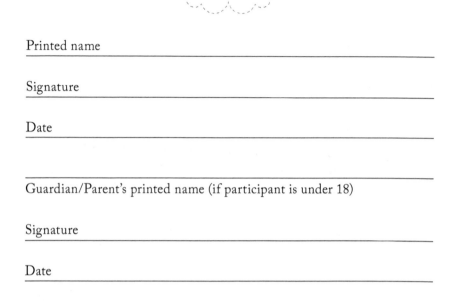

Printed name

Signature

Date

Guardian/Parent's printed name (if participant is under 18)

Signature

Date

I praise you (God) because I am fearfully and wonderfully made.
Psalm 139:14

IOHB Informed Consent/Group Commitment Form[7]

Goal and Time Commitment

The goal of the group is to enable its members to learn about identity in Christ, overcoming through Christ, healing through Christ, and bearing the image of Christ. Our intention is to teach, encourage, and provide prayer support for those members involved in the group. This group is not intended to be a counseling group.

By signing below, members are committing to attend and participate in all ten sessions of the group. If an absence is unavoidable, a group member must call her group administrator or facilitator in advance so they can plan accordingly. If a group member misses more than two sessions, the group administrator may decide to ask her to leave the current support group and rejoin a future group. It is important that all group members attend every meeting so that a sense of community and trust can be built within the group.

Facilitators

Your support group is a church-based ministry led by lay leaders who believe that a strong relationship with Jesus Christ is the foundation for a healthy, productive life. Your facilitators have gone through training and may have personally struggled with their own eating. However, they are not professional counselors. Indeed, the leader does not function in a therapeutic role, but as a support for growth. Professional boundaries are not as strict, but confidentiality is still absolutely vital. It is accepted that a facilitator will self-disclose at times and that she is still growing in her own maturity and recovery. The facilitator supports and encourages the group process by focusing on specific relational and spiritual needs. Members attend because they feel stress in coping with life's problems and/or desire emotional and spiritual growth and a fresh perspective from others.

Confidentiality

Confidentiality is a central ethical issue in groups. The leader of your support group has an ethical responsibility to maintain confidentiality, as does each group member. Thus, the leaders will not divulge any information concerning group members to family members or any other interested party unless the information shared meets the conditions mentioned in the "Exceptions to Confidentiality" section below. Confidentiality basically means that whatever is said in the group stays in the group. You can feel free to discuss with others what you personally have learned from the group, as well as anything you have shared with the group. However, you are not allowed to repeat anything that someone else has shared in the group. Neither are you allowed to disclose any personal information such as their name, where they live, or other statements that would allow someone else to identify them.

Exceptions to Confidentiality

There are some exceptions to confidentiality. If the facilitator or group administrator learns that you are in danger of hurting yourself or another person, he or she has a moral obligation to report such information to the proper authorities and other concerned parties without your permission or knowledge. These situations include, but may not be limited to, a member's purging or withholding of food on a daily basis, indications of bodily harm to others, suicidal intentions, and reasonable evidence of child abuse. If one of these occurs, it is required legally and ethically to inform the proper medical, law enforcement, and/or other concerned parties.

Informed Consent

By signing this document I agree that as a participant of IOHB, I understand and consent to participate in my support group. I understand that my facilitators are not professionals. In addition, I will adhere to the rules of confidentiality and understand the limitations of confidentiality. Should I violate the rule of confidentiality as defined above, I understand and agree

that the facilitator or group administrator has my permission to confront me using biblical models of confrontation, repentance, and restoration; and that they have the right to ask for my withdrawal from the present support group. I also understand that the IOHB leader(s) cannot prevent another group member from breaking confidentiality. I agree not to hold them, the author, One Degree Ministries, or any other IOHB representative(s) or lay leaders liable for any damage occurring from such an instance. I also hold the aforementioned parties harmless for the materials presented in this study and understand that healing from and overcoming my eating disorder is a process, and that the author, One Degree Ministries, or any other IOHB representative(s) or lay leaders have never promised instant and complete healing from my eating disorder tendencies upon completion of this study.

Group Member's Printed Name
_____

Group Member's Signature
_____

Date
_____

Parental/Guardian's Printed Name (if under 18)
_____

Signature
_____

Date
_____

Group Administrator's Printed Name
_____

Group Administrator's Signature
_____

Date
_____

Notes

1. Francis Chan, *Forgotten God* (Colorado Springs: David C. Cook, 2009), 103.

2. Beth Moore, *Praying God's Word* (Nashville: Broadman and Holman, 2000), 2–3.

3. Beth Moore, *Living Beyond Yourself* (Nashville: LifeWay Press, 2004), 214.

4. Nonie Maupin, CISW with Joan Webb, *The Head to Heart Card* (Scottsdale, 2004), 58.

5. It must be noted that this woman is different from the woman that anointed Jesus in Matthew 26:7, Mark 14:3, and John 12:3. Various commentators agree that there are two women who poured ointment on Jesus Christ. It is also important to note that the account we have studied happened towards the beginning of Jesus' public ministry. The other account, mentioned in Matthew, Mark, and John was performed by Mary, the sister of Lazarus, before Passover at the end of Jesus' earthly ministry.

6. Based on "Guide to Intake Form and Interview for Potential Group Participants," Mending the Soul Ministries: Facilitator Resource Guide, CD-ROM (Phoenix, AZ: Mending the Soul Ministries, 2009). Used with permission.

7. Based on "Informed Consent for MTS Support Groups," Mending the Soul Ministries: Facilitator Resource Guide, CD-ROM (Phoenix, AZ: Mending the Soul Ministries, 2009). Used with permission.

Made in the USA
San Bernardino, CA
29 January 2017